Be the Best
FRESHWATER FISHING

A Step-By-Step Guide

By Richard Smithsen

Troll Associates

Library of Congress Cataloging-in-Publication Data

Smithsen, Richard.
    Freshwater fishing: a step-by-step guide / by Richard Smithsen.
      p.   cm.—(Be the best!)
    Summary: Discusses how and where to fish, what kind of equipment to use, and what kinds of freshwater fishes can be caught.
      ISBN 0-8167-1941-1 (lib. bdg.)   ISBN 0-8167-1942-X (pbk.)
      1. Fishing—Juvenile literature. 2. Fishes, Fresh-water—Juvenile literature. [1. Fishing.] I. Title. II. Title: Freshwater fishing. III. Series.
SH445.S65   1990
799.1'1—dc20   89-20453

Copyright © 1990 by Troll Associates

All rights reserved. No part of this book may be used or reproduced in any manner whatsoever without written permission from the publisher.

Printed in the United States of America.

10 9 8 7 6 5 4 3 2

Be the Best
FRESHWATER FISHING

A Step-By-Step Guide

FOREWORD

by David Cutts

Fishing is one sport almost anyone can enjoy. It can be relaxing, exciting, refreshing, or challenging—as well as a lot of fun! I first discovered the joys of "angling" from my father, who used to take me with him when he went fishing. Sometimes we would sit for hours with our lines trailing off behind the boat, waiting patiently for that big one to bite...and sometimes we could barely catch our breath because the fish would bite as soon as the lures hit the water!

That's one of the great things about fishing: it can be different things at different times. You can battle a big-game fish until you finally land it. Or you can simply drop a line into the water and pull up a bottom feeder. (If you're lucky!)

No matter why you take up fishing, this book will help you learn the basics of freshwater fishing, including where to fish, how to fish, and what kinds of tackle and bait to use. *Freshwater Fishing, A Step-by-Step Guide,* can also help you identify the fish you catch, whether they're catfish or bass, perch or trout, pumpkinseed sunfish or bottom-dwelling carp. Just about the only thing it can't do is get the fish onto the hook. That part is up to you. And that's what makes fishing such challenging fun!

Contents

Chapter	Title	Page
1	Let's Go Fishing	7
2	What You Need to Fish	11
3	Arranging Your Equipment	23
4	Natural Bait	27
5	Prepared Bait	33
6	Artificial Bait	35
7	Still Fishing	39
8	Casting	47
9	Where and When to Fish	53
10	Some Freshwater Fish	55
11	Cleaning a Fish	61
12	Safe Fishing Fun	62

Let's Go Fishing

Do you want to try a sport that's simple, inexpensive, and a lot of fun? If you do, then what are you waiting for? Let's go fishing!

People who fish, or anglers as they are sometimes called, come in all shapes and sizes. They are young and old, male and female, big and small. Some take the sport of fishing very seriously. Others just fish for rest and relaxation. But no matter who they are, anglers have one thing in common. They all want to catch fish!

When it comes to fish, there are many different kinds to catch and many different ways to catch them. Did you know there are more than 15,000 different kinds of fish in the world? Some are surprisingly easy to catch. Others are harder to catch. To be successful, all it takes is patience, a little knowledge, and the right equipment.

What fishing equipment to use is up to you. You can go fishing with a rig that is inexpensive. Or if you have extra money, you can outfit yourself with slightly more expensive fishing gear. Either way, you can catch fish and have a good time.

In this book, you'll learn about fishing equipment and how to fish. You can get fishing equipment at your local sporting goods store. Buy the best equipment you can afford. If you take care of it, your fishing gear can last a long time and can be used over and over again.

Most people live within fairly easy traveling distance of a river, lake, or pond. Not everyone, however, can make it to the ocean. As a result, this book will focus on freshwater fishing rather than saltwater fishing. But keep in mind that some of the methods used to fish in fresh water can also be used to fish in salt water.

The most important thing to remember about fishing is that it's fun. It doesn't matter what kind of gear you use or where you fish. There is nothing like the thrill of hooking a good-sized fish.

Of course, there's never any guarantee you will catch a fish when you go fishing. Sometimes catching fish takes a little luck. But using the methods described in this book will teach you what you need to know to get started. The rest is up to you. Find a good fishing spot and be patient. Who knows? You just might hook the big one that *didn't* get away.

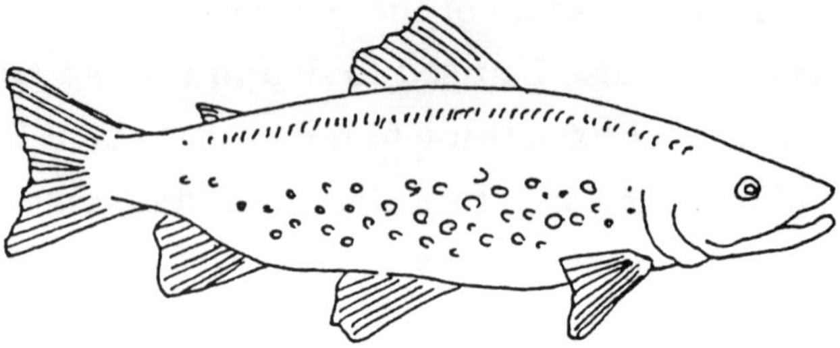

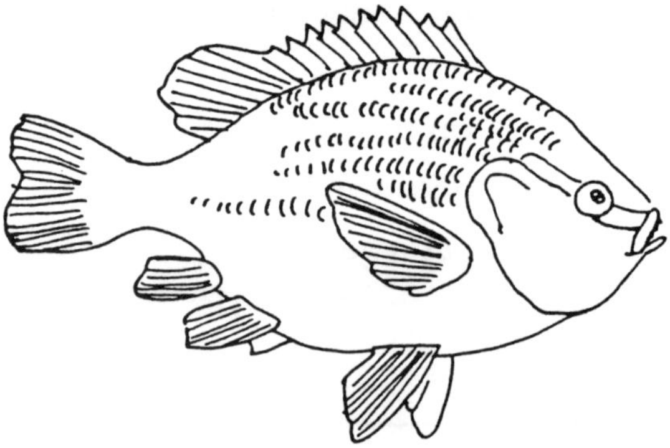

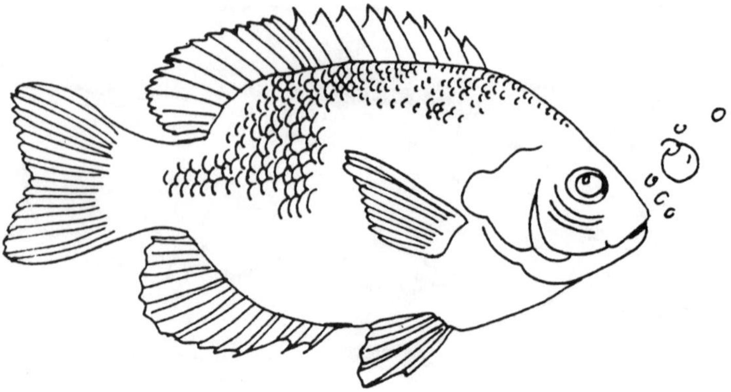

What You Need To Fish

Fishing equipment can be expensive or inexpensive. It depends on how much you have or want to spend. Most sporting goods stores have good fishing equipment for a reasonable price. But even with very little money to spend, you can get fishing equipment that will do the job.

FISHING LINE

Fishing line is a little like string, but it is much stronger. The difference between light fishing line and heavy fishing line is that light line breaks with fewer pounds of pressure than heavy line.

There are several kinds of fishing lines, each with its own test strength. If a line has a test strength of five pounds, for example, that means it will hold anything that pulls on it up to five pounds. More than five pounds of pressure will snap the line.

Beginning anglers should use light line that's strong enough to handle the size of fish they wish to catch. Basically, the lighter the line is, the more easily it tangles. The heavier the line is, the bulkier and harder it is to handle.

HOOKS

A hook is a curved piece of metal with a sharp point. Hooks come in many sizes, and hook sizes have numbers. The smaller the number is, the larger the hook is. For example, a number one hook is a big hook.

A hook is made up of several parts. The *eye* is where the hook is attached to the line. The *shank* is the long straight part of the hook. The *bend* is the curved part of the hook, and the *point* and the *barb* are the sharp parts. The *gap* of the hook is the distance from the shank to the point. The *bite* is the distance from the point's tip to the lowest part of the bend.

Different kinds of hooks have been designed to make catching different kinds of fish easier. When buying hooks, ask for those that are good for catching perch, sunfish, bass, or whatever.

THE FISHING HOOK

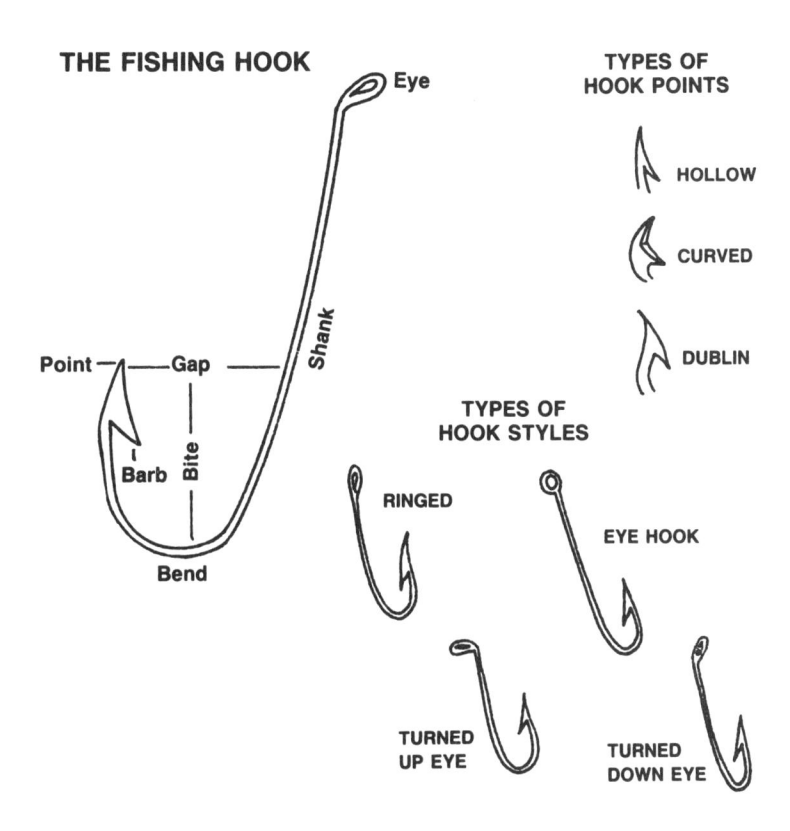

TYPES OF HOOK POINTS
- HOLLOW
- CURVED
- DUBLIN

TYPES OF HOOK STYLES
- RINGED
- EYE HOOK
- TURNED UP EYE
- TURNED DOWN EYE

Hook parts labeled: Eye, Shank, Point, Gap, Barb, Bite, Bend

Hooks sometimes come three or four in a package and already tied to nylon monofilament leader. These are called snelled hooks.

Whatever kind of hooks you buy, it's easy to stick yourself with a fishhook. Please be careful!

LEADER

A leader is a short length of wire, monofilament, nylon coated wire, or some other material. It can be used to connect the fishing line with the hook.

SINKERS

A sinker is a lead weight that helps drop the hook and line deeper in the water. Sinkers come in many shapes, sizes, and weights.

Very popular sinkers that can be attached and removed easily are split shot sinkers. They are little round lead balls that are partially sliced through. To attach them, you just put the line in the slice openings and then squeeze the shots between your fingers around the line. The splits will close, sealing the shots to the line.

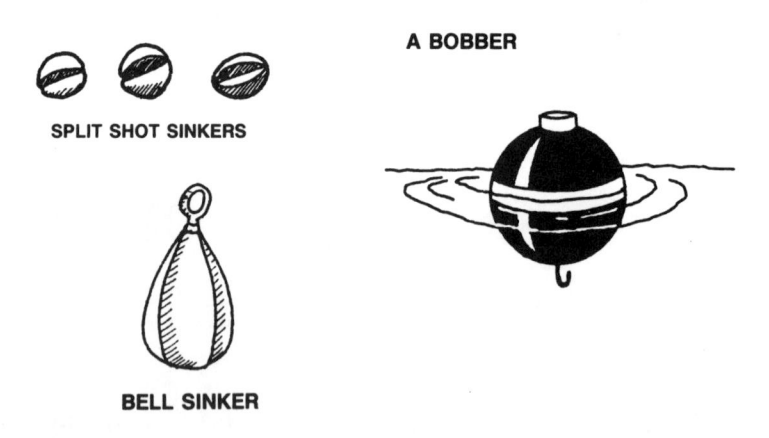

SPLIT SHOT SINKERS

A BOBBER

BELL SINKER

BOBBERS

The bobber is attached to the line above the leader. This way, the bobber will float on the surface of the water while the baited hook dangles just below. The bobber helps an angler know when a fish is after the bait. When the bobber jerks, moves around, or dips underwater, a fish has taken the bait. A bobber also controls the depth of your bait. If you move the bobber up the line your bait will go deeper in the water.

SWIVELS AND SNAPS

A swivel can be used to join a hook or leader to the end of the fishing line. When the hook is being drawn through the water, the swivel turns instead of the line. A snap makes the attachment of leaders and hooks much easier.

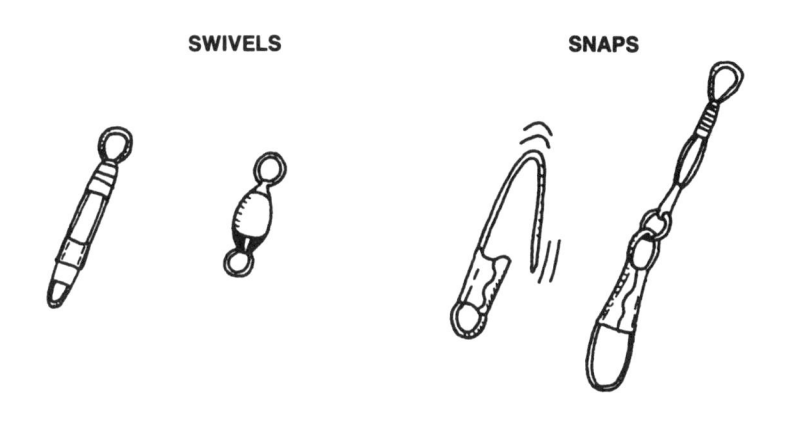

SWIVELS **SNAPS**

PALOMAR KNOT

There may be times when you will have to tie a hook to your line. A simple knot that works very well is the *Palomar knot*.

Start with plenty of line. Double the line and pass the end through the hook's eye. Tie an overhand knot with the two loose ends of the line (like you were tying your shoe strings), but do not pull it tight yet. Pass the hook through the loop in the doubled end of the line. Pull the loose end of line to tighten the knot. Trim the end. Leave at least 1/8 inch of your line at the knot.

PALOMAR KNOT

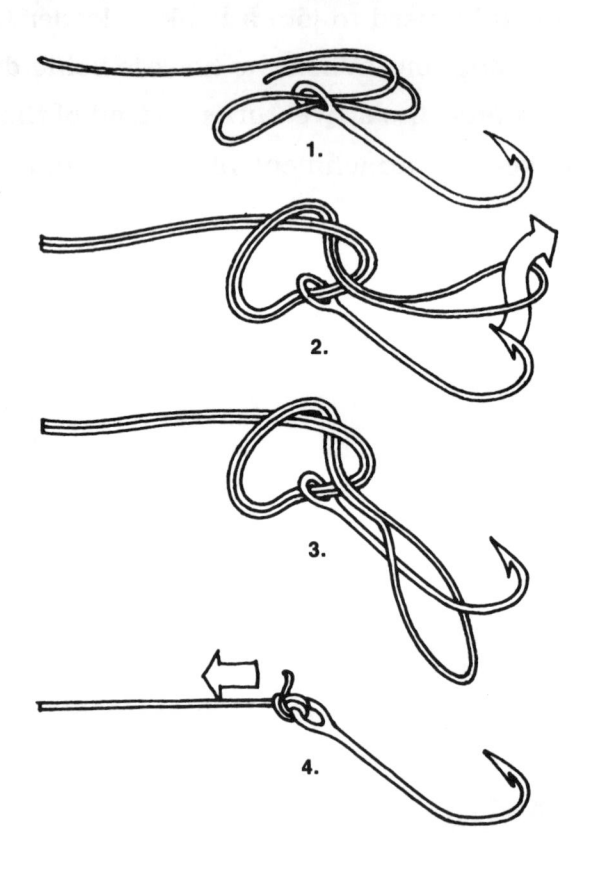

HAND LINES

A hand line is a simple and cheap way to fish. A hand line comes complete with a line, a hook, and a sinker and/or a bobber. In simple terms, a hand line is fishing line wound around a large metal or wooden spool.

To use a hand line, you just bait the hook, unwind some line, and toss it in the water. Hand lines are good for fishing close to the shore.

RODS AND POLES

Anglers normally use a pole or rod. Rods are usually shorter than poles, and are normally used with reels to cast bait away from the angler. Poles are longer, and aren't used for casting.

POLES

Poles are long, straight lengths made of cane, bamboo, or even a flexible tree branch. Many anglers consider bamboo the best material for a pole. You can either make a pole or buy one in a sporting goods store. Store-bought poles come in various lengths. Some are eight feet long, while others are twelve or more feet long. The longer the pole is, the farther out in the water you can reach with your line. Pole fishing is usually done at the water's edge or off a dock or pier.

Once you have your pole, tie a length of fishing line to the thinner end of the pole. You can decide which test strength (see page 12) to use based on the type of fish you are after. Next, attach your other equipment to the line (see pages 24-25 for instructions).

REELS

A reel is a spool around which fishing line is wrapped. There are many different kinds of reels. But all reels have a handle or crank on the side that rewinds line on the spool after you throw, or cast, the line.

CLOSE-FACE SPIN-CASTING REEL

The close-face spin-casting reel is probably the best one for beginners. It is simple and usually trouble free, and it does not tangle easily. It is also inexpensive.

The close-face spin-casting reel looks like a cone-shaped can. The fishing line comes out of a hole in the cone end and is fed down the length of the rod.

At the other end of the reel is a thumb button. Pressing it will release the line and allow you to cast the line out in the water.

On one side of the reel is a handle for winding the line on the reel. This also pulls the line in. Turning the handle automatically resets the thumb button. Reeling in the line is called the *retrieve* in fishing. A spin-casting reel is used with a casting rod. As you hold the rod, the reel rests on top of the rod.

CLOSE-FACE SPIN-CASTING REEL

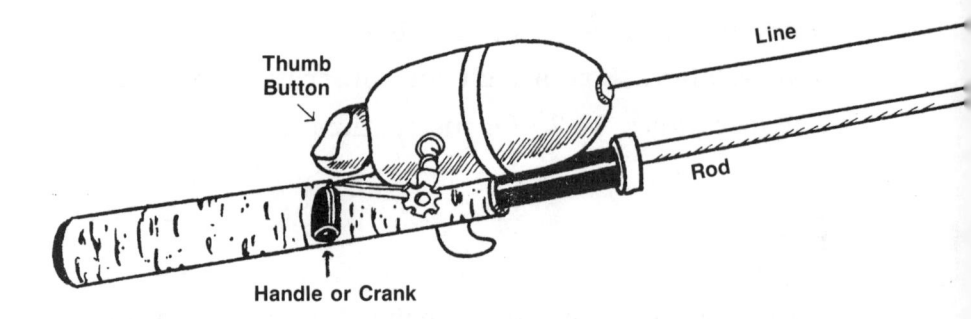

OPEN-FACE SPINNING REEL

An open-face spinning reel is a spin-casting reel without a cone cover. It has a thin metal loop around half of the reel's top that is called a *reel bail*. As you reel in the line, the bail revolves and guides it onto the spool during the retrieve (see page 18). The spool of an open-face spinning reel does not turn or spin itself. In order to cast, the bail must be flipped down while you use your finger to prevent the line from drooping.

Spinning reels are used with spinning rods. The spinning reel hangs *under* the rod on a straight handle. This reel is not recommended for beginners.

OPEN-FACE SPINNING REEL

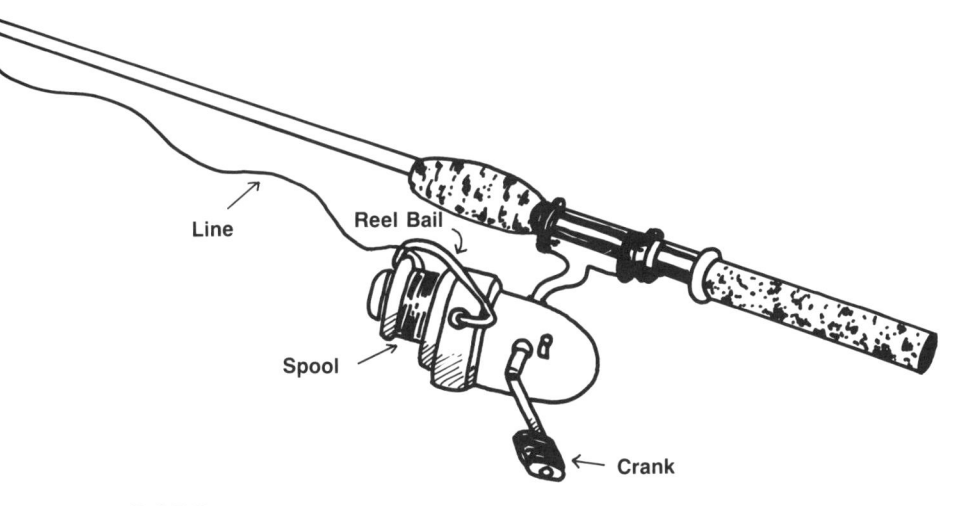

RODS

Today, most fishing rods are made of graphite or fiber glass. The grip is the thick part of the pole held in the hand. It is usually padded with cork or other material. There is a groove cut into the rod where you place the reel and then lock it into place. It is called the *reel seat*. With casting rods, the back of the reel seat has a finger hook or rest.

Down the length of the pole and at the tip are little guides for threading the fishing line. The line goes from the reel, down through all the loops, and the hook is fastened at the end.

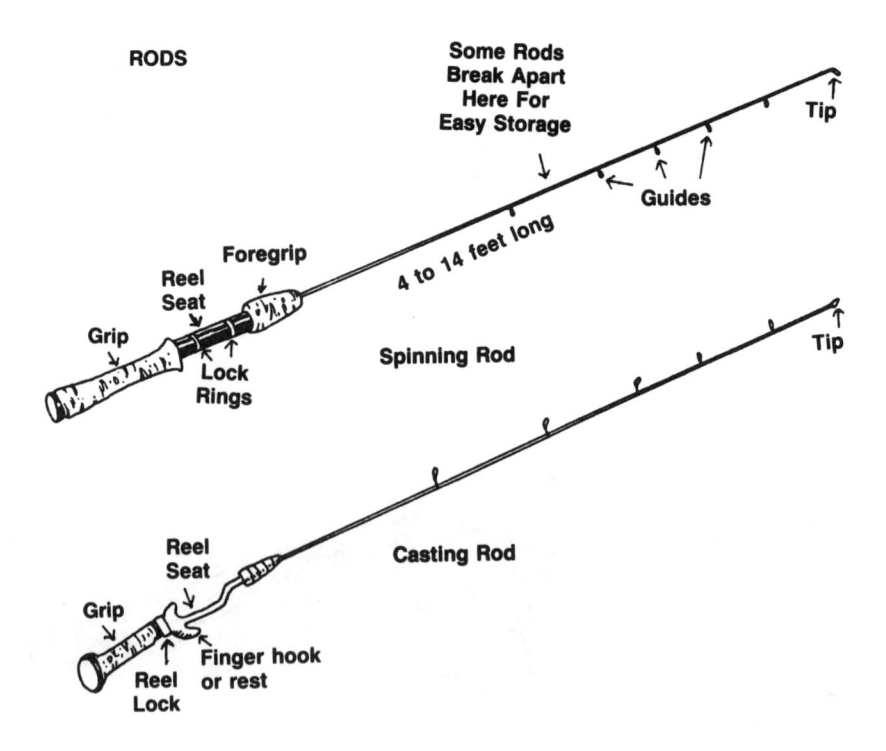

RODS

Some Rods Break Apart Here For Easy Storage

Tip

Foregrip

Reel Seat

Grip

Lock Rings

4 to 14 feet long

Guides

Spinning Rod

Tip

Reel Seat

Grip

Reel Lock

Finger hook or rest

Casting Rod

Most fishing rods come apart into two sections for easy storage. A spinning rod is usually five to seven feet long, and a casting rod is three to six and a half feet long. You should probably start with a lightweight casting rod four and a half to five and a half feet long.

BALANCED TACKLE

Your rod, reel and line and the kind of bait you use need to match each other. This is called balanced tackle. For example, you put a light-action reel with a light-action rod. You put lighter line on a light reel and heavy line on a larger heavy-duty reel. Use lighter line when using smaller baits, heavier line when using large heavy baits.

Have a salesperson who knows about fishing help you to select what is best for you.

TACKLE BOX

A tackle box will help you organize your fishing gear. It is just a plastic or metal box with several levels that are divided into small compartments.

NEEDLE-NOSE PLIERS

Keeping an ordinary pair of needle-nose pliers in your tackle box is a good idea. Pliers are handy for removing hooks from fish.

NET

Although not absolutely necessary, a hand net makes landing fish much easier. You scoop them up out of the water from underneath.

FISHING REGULATIONS

All states have fishing regulations. Know how many fish you are allowed to keep and whether there is a size limit.

Almost all states in the United States require a license to fish in fresh water. Usually, however, youngsters under the age of thirteen or fourteen do not need a license. But it's best to check out your state's fishing laws before you go fishing.

BAIT

Another essential part of any fishing gear is bait. This is what you use to get fish to bite. Fish are likely to be attracted to a bait that looks like or is a part of their usual diet. Using the right bait is one of the secrets to catching fish. The three different kinds of bait—natural, prepared, and artificial—are discussed in detail on pages 27-38.

Arranging Your Equipment

Most rods and reels are sold as sets, with line already wound on the reel. If a reel is sold separately, it will more often than not have line on it. If it doesn't, get an adult or a store salesclerk to wind the line on the reel for you.

If you buy a rod and reel separately, put your reel in the reel seat (see page 20). Make sure the reel stays in place by loosening the locking device and then retightening it.

Next, feed line out of the reel and thread it through the guides (rings) on the rod. If your rod comes in two sections, connect the sections first. Once the line is threaded through the final guide, you can move to the finishing touches.

PREPARING EQUIPMENT

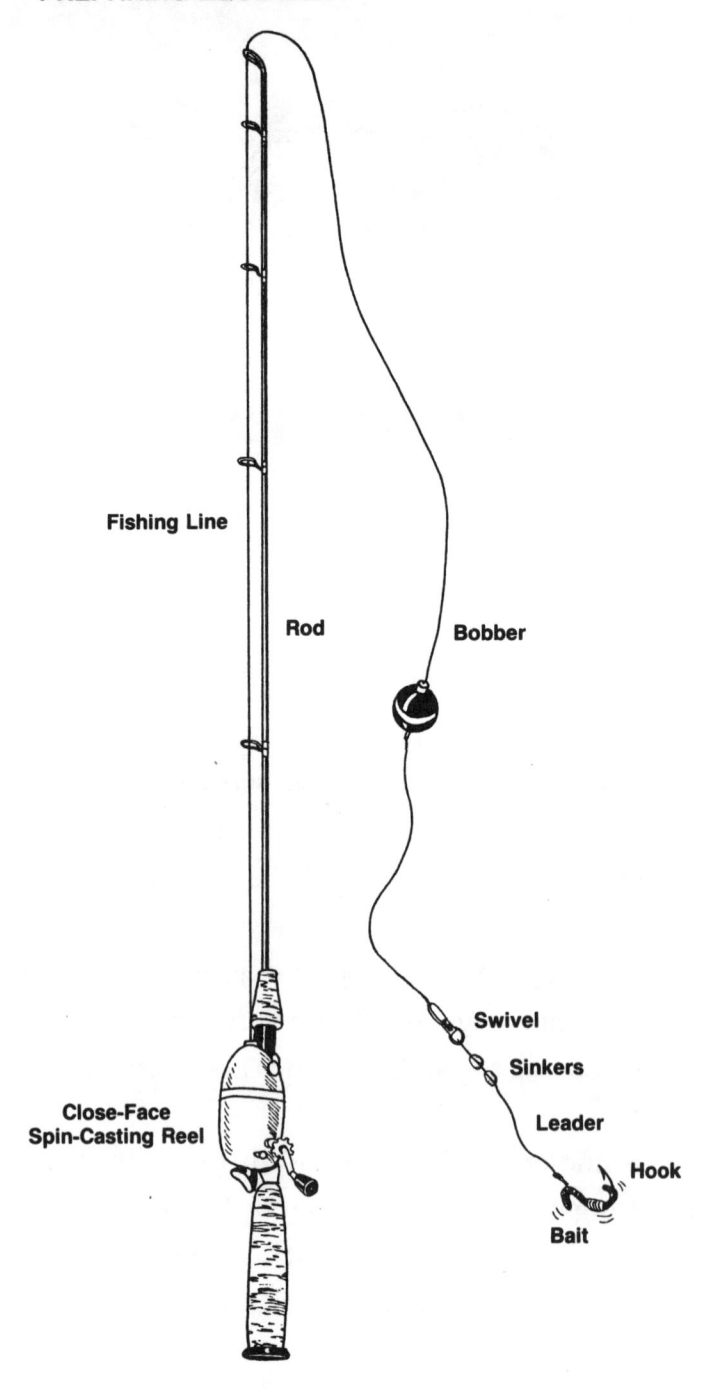

Fishing Line

Rod

Bobber

Close-Face
Spin-Casting Reel

Swivel

Sinkers

Leader

Hook

Bait

Whether you have a rod and reel rig or a pole, these instructions will help you get your equipment ready for fishing. Attach a bobber to your line. Remember that the closer the bobber is to the pole or rod end of your line, the deeper the hook will go in the water. Attach split shot sinkers nearer the free end of the line. Then, *carefully* tie a hook to the end of your line, using a Palomar knot (see pages 15-16).

Another technique is to attach a snelled hook (see page 13) to the end of the line by using a swivel or a snap. Make sure to use a Palomar knot .

You're almost ready to fish now. All you need to do next is get the right bait and hook it. You can use natural, prepared, or artificial bait.

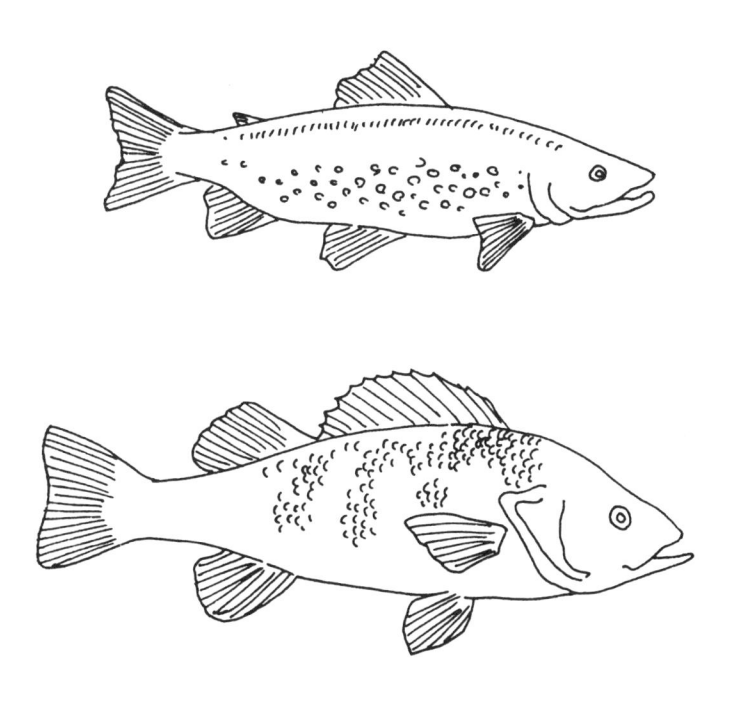

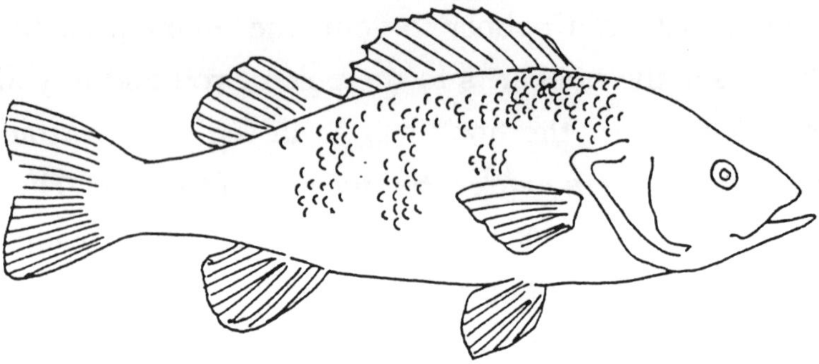

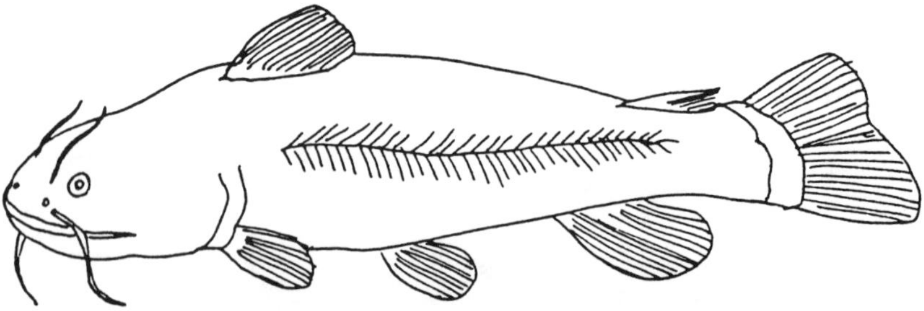

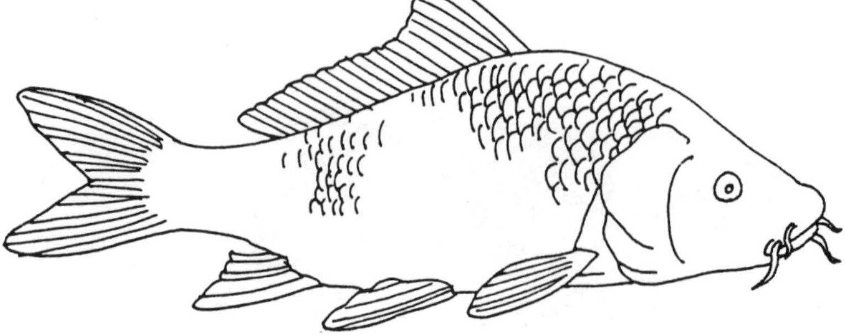

4

Natural Bait

This is bait that is or was alive. Natural bait can be caught, dug up, or sometimes bought at sporting goods stores. It includes worms, grasshoppers, crickets, and minnows.

WORMS

Believe it or not, plain wiggly worms are still the best all-around bait available for fishing. Almost all freshwater fish will be attracted to and bite on worms.

When you plan a fishing trip, it's wise to hunt for worms the day before you go fishing. Dig under grassy areas or in shady spots where the soil is firm but not baked hard. Turn clumps of dirt over with a shovel or spade and then break the clumps apart to find the worms. Worms of all sizes and shapes are good. Place them in an open-ended container with a little dirt and keep them out of the sun.

Night crawlers also make excellent bait. They are long, flat worms that come out of the ground at night. Sprinkling a good amount of water on the lawn in the afternoon will help get night crawlers to come out after dark.

After you've found enough worms, keep them in a cool place until you go fishing. If you can't dig or find worms, you can always buy some at a sporting goods store.

How should you bait a hook with a worm? *Carefully!* Remember that hooks are sharp. There are several ways to bait a worm on a hook, and they all work. You might even develop your own special way for baiting a worm.

The basics for baiting a worm, however, have not changed much. Slide your hook through the middle of the worm, keeping the hook's point inside the worm's body. Allow the ends of the worm to dangle free at the shank of the hook and the point. Hooked properly, a worm will wiggle in the water for fifteen to twenty minutes. The worm's motion is what attracts the fish.

Smaller fish will go after small worms and even bits of worms stuck on the point of the hook. Bigger fish are attracted to big worms or several worms stuck on the same hook. When putting more than one worm on a hook, make sure the ends of all the worms dangle free. Again, it is the wiggling of the worms that brings the fish to the bait.

WAYS TO BAIT A WORM

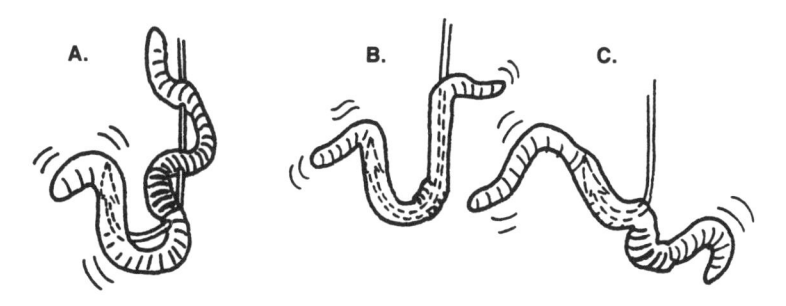

A. B. C.

WAYS TO BAIT MORE THAN ONE WORM

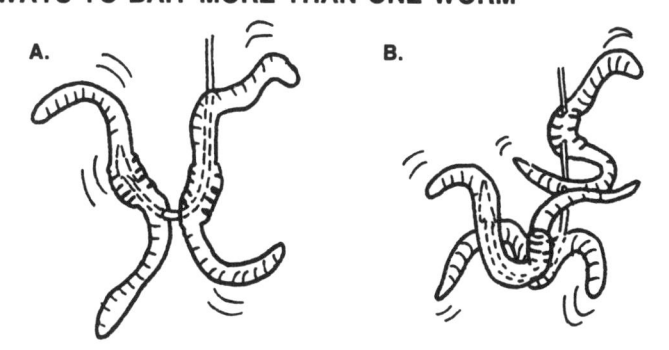

A. B.

GRASSHOPPERS AND CRICKETS

Grasshoppers and crickets are natural food for most fish. You can find them in almost any field or lawn. They can also be bought at bait stores and many sporting goods stores.

Grasshoppers and crickets can be baited several ways. Some people hook a grasshopper or cricket from the back, sticking the hook in the middle of the bug's back and bringing the point out behind its head (see diagram).

Other people hook a cricket or grasshopper by sticking the hook in behind the bug's head so the point emerges through the middle of the bug's back.

WAYS TO BAIT GRASSHOPPERS AND CRICKETS

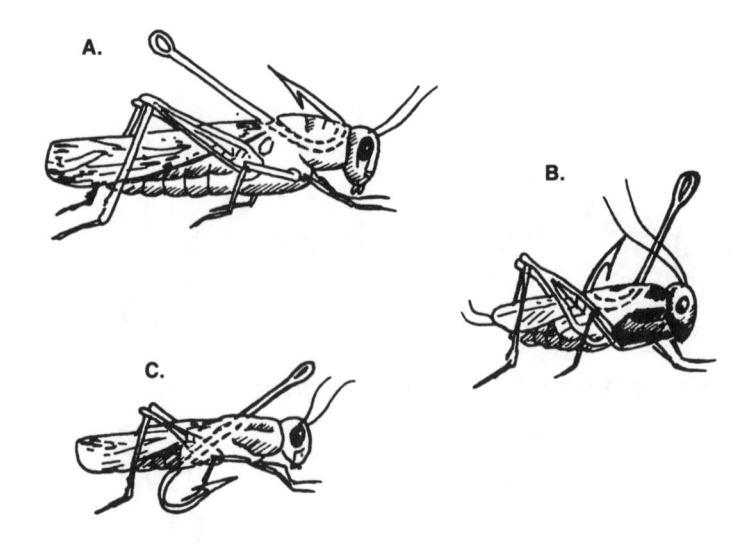

A.

B.

C.

Still other anglers like to put a small hook through the entire body of the bug so the point emerges near the end and faces frontward under the bug.

MINNOWS

Minnows are very small fish found mostly in creeks, streams, brooks, and ponds. Minnows can be caught by using special nets or traps, or you can buy live or dead minnows at a bait store.

Special containers for minnows are sold but you can put them in any kind of bucket. Just remember to keep their water cool and fresh.

Live minnows swim around and attract the larger fish like bass. To keep a minnow alive while using it as bait, hook the minnow through the lips so the point of the hook faces away from the minnow. You can also hook the minnow in the middle of the back from the side. Hook the minnow just in front of its back fin.

WAYS TO BAIT MINNOWS

LIVE MINNOWS

A. Through Lips

B. Through Back

A DEAD MINNOW

Thread Line Through Its Body

A dead minnow can be hooked by threading the hook through its body in a sewing fashion. It can be hooked through the mouth and out the side, and then rehooked just in front of the tail.

Prepared Bait

This is bait you can mix up on your own in the kitchen. Prepared bait includes bread paste or dough balls, and cheesy chunks.

BREAD PASTE OR DOUGH BALLS

It's easy to make dough balls. Cut the crusts off slices of bread. Let the bread soak in cold water for a few minutes. Put the soggy bread in a cloth and squeeze it until most of the water is out and the bread gets pasty. The paste is what you use for bait.

Take a piece of the bread paste and roll it into a dough ball. Put the dough ball on your hook. Make sure it is big enough to fit over the hook's point. Big fish such as carp and catfish especially like dough balls.

LINE BAITED WITH DOUGH BALL

CHEESY CHUNKS

Mix old sharp cheese with honey and flour. Mold it in your hands until it is pasty. Then roll bits of it into bait-size chunks. Put them on your hook the same way you did the dough balls. Catfish, in particular, find cheesy chunks a tasty snack.

Artificial Bait

Artificial bait is manmade. It looks like natural bait and often imitates the motion of live bait in the water. Artificial bait is meant to attract fish and then trick them into biting it. Different kinds of artificial bait are also called lures.

A regular hook isn't needed because the lures themselves have a hook. A special casting and retrieving technique is used with most artificial bait. Popular lures include flies, plugs, jigs, spoons, spinners, and spinnerbaits.

FLIES

These are used mostly for trout fishing. But bass and small fish such as bluegills (see page 56) also take flies. Flies are just pieces of feathers, hair, and other material skillfully tied to look like an insect or insect larva. They come already tied to the hooks and are used instead of natural bait.

There are two kinds of flies: wet and dry. A wet fly is made so that it will sink as soon as it hits the water after a cast. Wet flies are best when used in rough or running water. A dry fly is made so that it will float high on top of the water. Dry flies are best when used in clear, cool, quiet pools.

TWO TYPES OF DRY FLIES

Bumblebee   White Miller

TWO TYPES OF WET FLIES

Loop Wing Emerger   Sandy Mite

PLUGS

These are usually made of wood or plastic and look like small fish or frogs. Some plugs float on the surface; others stay underwater. Plugs usually have multiple hooks, with each hook cluster made up of three points. Plugs can be used for many kinds of fish.

PLUGS

JIGS

A jig is just a hook with a molded lead head which acts as a sinker. They are made in all kinds of sizes and shapes. Small jigs are good for perch while larger jigs are good for bass and other big fish. Jigs almost always are "dressed" with live or artificial bait, which is attached to the hook.

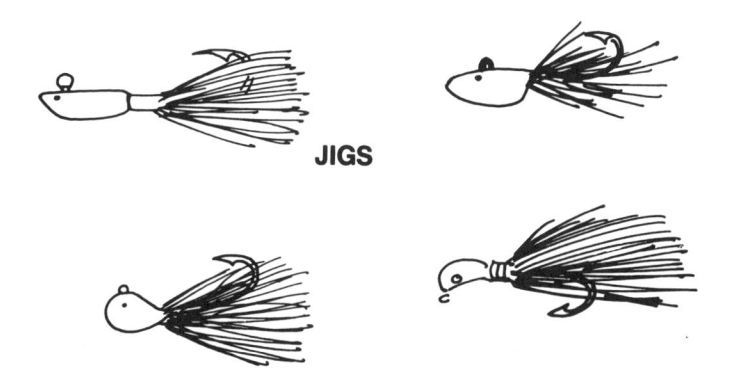

JIGS

SPOONS, SPINNERS, AND SPINNERBAITS

Spoons are made of shiny metal and are excellent fish foolers. Where did the name for this lure come from? Well, it looks somewhat like a spoon. But an old fishing tale suggests another reason. One day, a fisherman was eating lunch when he accidentally dropped his shiny spoon into the water. A whopping big fish swam by and snapped at it. Ever since then, spoons have been popular among anglers everywhere.

Spinners and spinnerbaits have thin metal blades that spin in the water like propellers. Sometimes they have feathers on their hooks. Most spinners and spoons use multiple, three-pointed hooks. Spinnerbaits usually have one hook.

SPOON

SPINNER

SPINNERBAIT

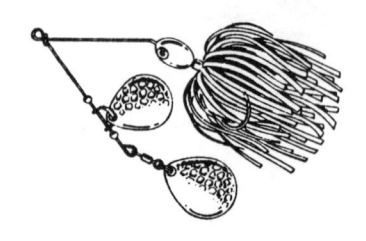

Still Fishing

Still fishing is probably the easiest way for you to begin the sport of fishing. Later, you can move on to other, more advanced fishing techniques.

Still fishing means you place a baited line in the water, leave it in one place, and wait for a fish to bite. There are two ways to still fish. You can fish using a bobber, which dangles your bait at one level or another below the surface. Or you can fish along the bottom, using sinkers but no bobber.

The easiest way to start still fishing is with a bobber. Using a bobber, you can fish at different depths. If you are fishing near the shallow shore, put your bobber on the line closer to the hook (see page 14). If you are fishing in a deeper area, place the bobber higher up on the line. Try to get your bait to hang in the water above the bottom but not too close to the surface.

Swing or toss your line into the water. Your bobber will float. This is your fish indicator. Watch it carefully. You can hold your pole or rod, lay it on the bank near the water, or put it in a pole holder. A pole holder is just a Y-shaped tree branch or metal pole. The straight part of the pole holder goes into the ground. Rest your pole or rod in the Y groove so that the tip is elevated. That makes it easy to watch your line.

STILL FISHING

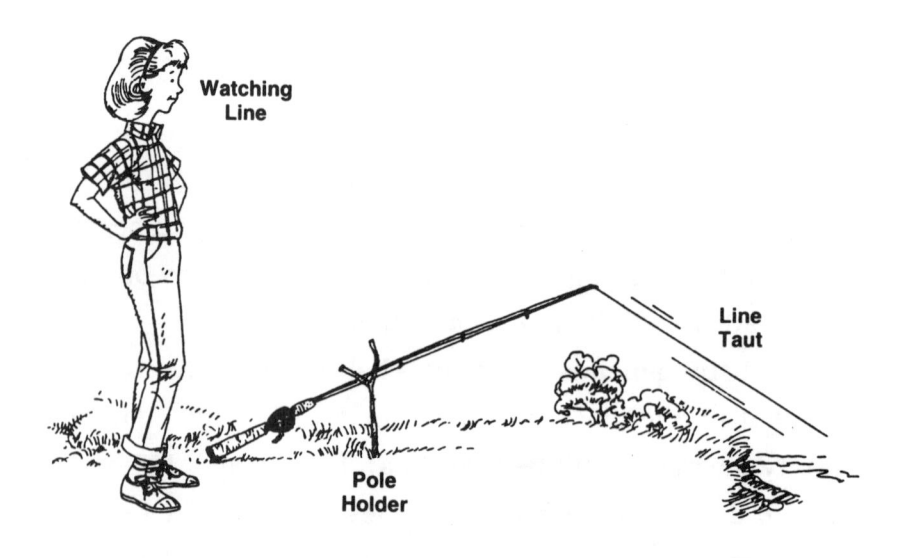

If the line from your rod to the bobber is too loose, turn the reel crank a bit to make the line straighter and tighter. If you're fishing with a pole, you don't have to worry about that.

If a fish starts to nibble at your bait, the bobber will jerk or bounce in the water. That is your signal to pick up your pole or rod if you are not holding it. Pick it up slowly and gently. When the bobber dips underwater, it means the fish has taken the bait into its mouth.

Now it's time for action, angler! You have to catch or hook the fish securely. That's called "setting the hook." Set the hook by flipping your pole or rod upward quickly but lightly.

SETTING THE HOOK

After you set the hook and have the fish on the line, start "playing the fish." This means letting the fish move the line and pole or rod in the direction it wants to go. Do not jerk the line out of the water or reel it in just yet, but *always* keep tension on the line.

Some anglers automatically reel the fish in after it's hooked. That is okay, but it takes some of the fun out of fishing. While you're playing a fish, it might jump out of the water, which can be a thrilling sight. If you plan to release the fish once you catch it, do not play the fish for too long.

PLAYING THE FISH

Bring The Line In By Raising The Rod's Tip

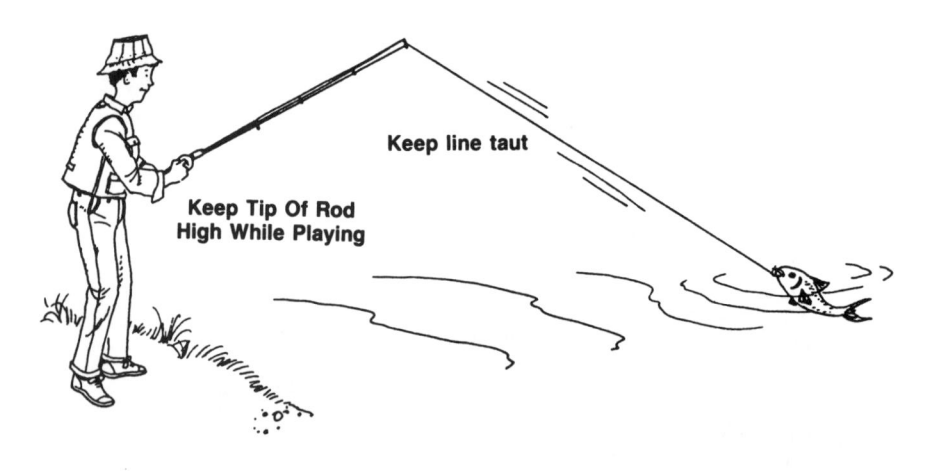

Keep line taut

Keep Tip Of Rod High While Playing

Keep the tip of your rod or pole high while playing a fish. Bring the line in by raising your pole's tip a little higher. That is all you have to do if you're using a pole. If you're using a reel, raise the tip of the rod and keep the line tight as you reel. Slightly lower your rod's tip and raise it again as you continue to retrieve. Bring the fish in slowly, keeping the tip of your fishing pole or rod up and the line taut. If you let the line go slack, the fish might slip off the hook.

Keep the tip of your rod up as the fish nears the shore or boat. At this point, you'll be "landing the fish," which means taking it out of the water. Here's where a hand net can help if you have one. Lower the net into the water and guide the fish into it headfirst. Avoid netting a fish tail first. When the fish is in the net, lift it out. Never lift a fish completely out of the water and then net him.

You can also bring the fish to the shore's edge, reach down into the water with your free hand, and take it out.

LANDING THE FISH

Fish May Wiggle Off If You Do This

Bring Fish To Bank And Lift Out

STILL FISHING ALONG THE BOTTOM

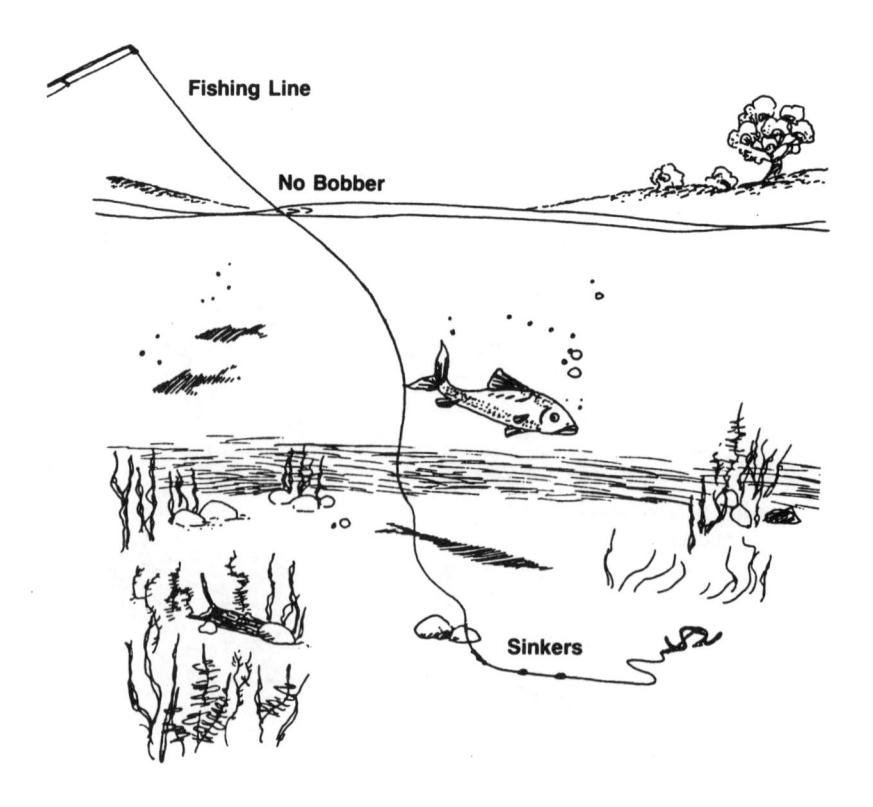

To still fish along the bottom, remove any bobber from your line. But make sure you have sinkers on it. You want your line to go all the way to the bottom. So after you bait your hook, toss or swing it into the water, giving it enough line to hit the bottom. If you're using a pole, you will have to dip the tip lower or fish in a shallow spot. If using a reel, give the line lots of slack until your bait reaches the bottom.

STILL FISHING ALONG THE BOTTOM

Once you feel the line hit bottom, you can either hold your rod or pole or place it on the ground or in a pole holder. Again, you want your line to stay taut. Do not let loose line float on the surface of the water. If your line is too slack after the bait hits bottom, hold your pole up or slightly retrieve your line on a reel by turning the crank. Once the line is taut, you're set.

Watching the taut line is how you'll know if a fish is interested in your bait. When the line starts to quiver or shake, that means a fish is nibbling on your bait. If you're not holding your rod or pole at this point, gently pick it up. A tug or jerk on the line means the fish has taken the bait. Now set the hook as described earlier (see page 41). Follow the same directions for fishing with a bobber to play and land your fish (see pages 41-43).

Still fishing along the bottom is a little harder than using a bobber. Beginners sometimes forget to watch the line as closely as they would a bobber. It is also a bit more difficult to know just when to set the hook. However, fishing along the bottom often hooks bigger fish such as carp (see page 55) and catfish (see page 57).

REMOVING HOOKS

Some hooks are very easy to remove, while others are much harder. Hooks caught in the lip or the edge of a fish's mouth are usually not too difficult to get out. But hooks in big fish, in fish with sharp teeth, or deep in a fish's mouth can be a problem.

You can remove most hooks from small fish without sharp teeth by sliding your forefinger as far as possible down the shank of the hook and then giving the hook a hard, quick push downward. That usually gets the barb and point free, letting you pull the hook out easily.

To remove hooks from big fish or fish with sharp teeth, use the needle-nose pliers in your tackle box to work the hooks loose. If the hook is too deep just cut the line and tie on another hook.

Before you fish, decide whether you are going to keep the fish. Never waste fish. Keep what you can eat and release the rest. If you plan to release the fish handle it as little as possible and return it to the water immediately. You can take the time to take a photograph of your catch.

8

Casting

Casting is a special way of accurately tossing your line out into the water. To cast, you need a rod and a reel.

Generally in casting, an angler throws a lure or bait to a place in the water where he or she thinks fish are swimming. The angler then reels the bait or lure back in a way that makes the fish think it's something good to eat. In this way, the angler lures the fish to the bait.

The best cast for beginners to learn and master is the basic overhead cast. Casting can be practiced in a big open area such as a field or lawn before attempting to cast while fishing.

A beginner's rod should have either a close-face spin-casting reel or an open-face spinning reel (see pages 17-19). Each reel requires a special method for casting.

OVERHEAD CASTING WITH A CLOSE-FACE REEL

If you're using a close-face spin-casting reel on your rod, hold it in your hand with the button facing up. Your thumb should be on the reel at the thumb button. If your rod has a finger hook, you can put your finger on it. Now move the rod up and down in front of you a few times to get the feel of the rod's action.

Once you feel comfortable, try an actual cast. If you are practicing in an open field, just use a practice plug (a plastic or rubber plug without hooks) on the end of the

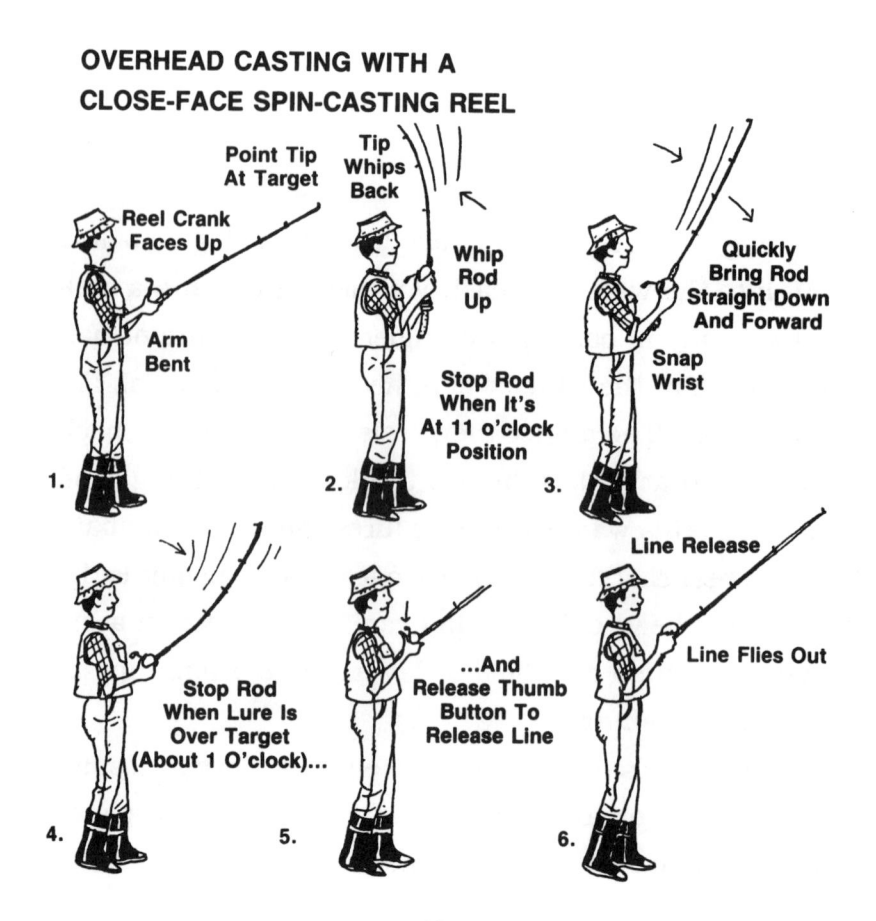

OVERHEAD CASTING WITH A CLOSE-FACE SPIN-CASTING REEL

1. Reel Crank Faces Up — Point Tip At Target — Arm Bent
2. Tip Whips Back — Whip Rod Up — Stop Rod When It's At 11 o'clock Position
3. Quickly Bring Rod Straight Down And Forward — Snap Wrist
4. Stop Rod When Lure Is Over Target (About 1 O'clock)...
5. ...And Release Thumb Button To Release Line
6. Line Release — Line Flies Out

48

line. *Never* use a hook. Always look behind you before you cast so you won't hit someone.

Hold the rod out in front of you. Keep it away from your body, with the tip raised about chin high and pointed at your target. Your arm should be slightly bent and your elbow should be close to your body. Put your thumb on the button and hold it in. Next, bring the rod straight back until it is just past your head. It's best to start from an eleven o'clock position and then adjust, depending on how much action your rod has and how far you intend to cast. Keep facing and looking at your target.

After you take the rod back, quickly bring it straight down and forward by snapping your wrist. As the rod tip comes forward, release the thumb button to release the line. Your rod should stop at about the same angle where you started or when the lure is just over your target.

Letting go of the thumb button when you should is a matter of good timing. If you let up on the upswing, the lure will shoot out behind you. If your line shoots up into the air, you released the thumb button too soon. If the lure is driven into the ground or water in front of you, you released the button too late. If your line went straight but fell short of your target, take your rod further back next time and bring it forward with a little more force.

When you hit your target with the lure, wait for it to settle. Then turn the reel crank to reset the thumb button. The line will lock. Now you can retrieve the lure.

OVERHEAD CASTING WITH AN OPEN-FACE REEL

To cast with an open-face spinning reel, you must first flip down the bail with your free hand. That lets the line loose. The way you keep the line taut is by holding it between your forefinger and the rod. Do not, however, pin the line against the rod with your forefinger. The pressure of your finger on the line will keep it from unwinding before casting.

As you're about to cast with an open-face spinning reel, hold the rod so that the reel is facing down at your feet underneath the rod. Your hand should grip the rod right where the reel is attached, with your forefinger holding the line. Your thumb should be on the rod, your middle finger in front of the metal attachment between rod and reel, and your remaining fingers behind this attachment. There is no finger hook on a spinning rod. And remember, your forefinger is what holds the line and keeps it from falling when the bail is down.

HOLDING AN OPEN-FACE SPINNING REEL TO CAST

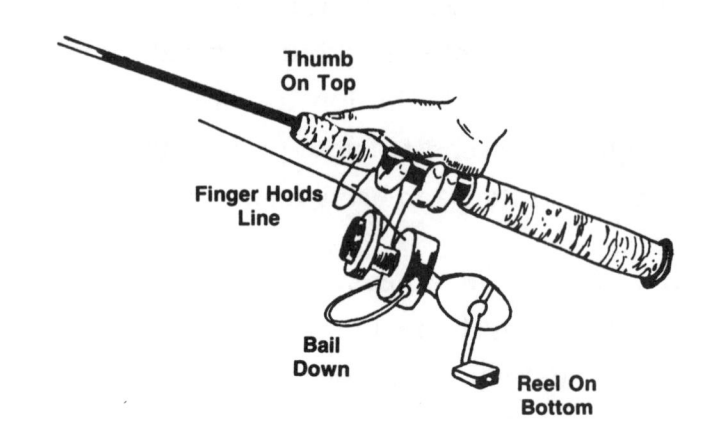

OVERHEAD CASTING WITH AN OPEN-FACE SPINNING REEL

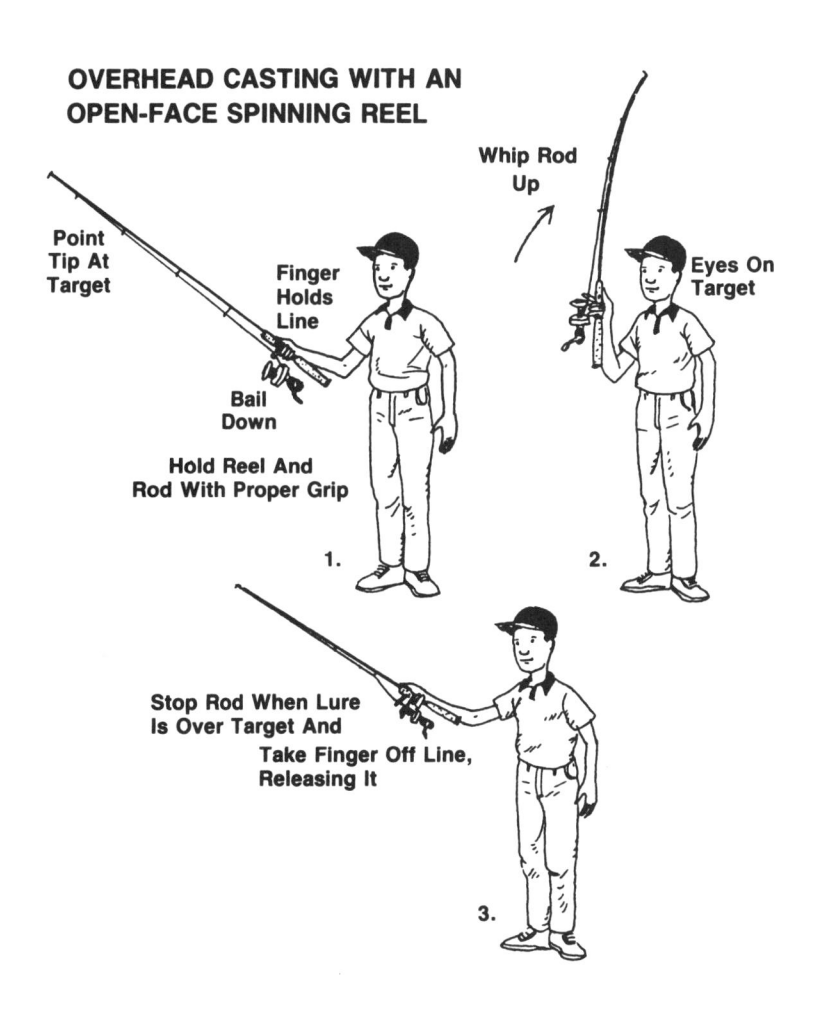

1.
- Point Tip At Target
- Finger Holds Line
- Bail Down
- Hold Reel And Rod With Proper Grip

2.
- Whip Rod Up
- Eyes On Target

3.
- Stop Rod When Lure Is Over Target And Take Finger Off Line, Releasing It

Now do a basic overhead cast as described on pages 48-49. Aim at your target. Bring the rod straight up and back so that it stops just past your head. As the tip bends back start your downward wrist snap. When the lure is just above your target on the downward whip, stop the rod and release the line held by your forefinger. Timing is once again important here. When you hit your target, rewind. Turning the crank automatically puts the winding bail back up on most open-face spinning reels.

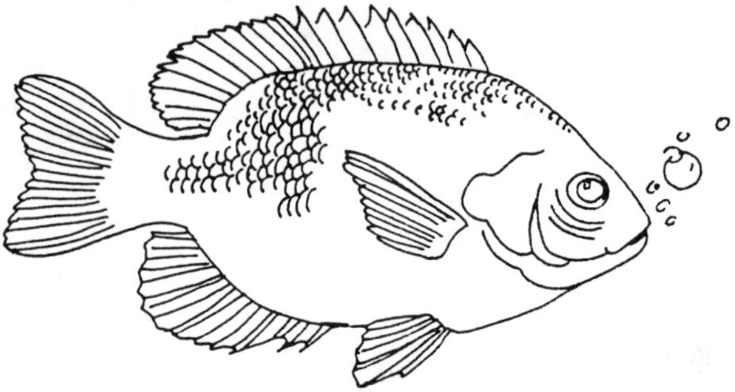

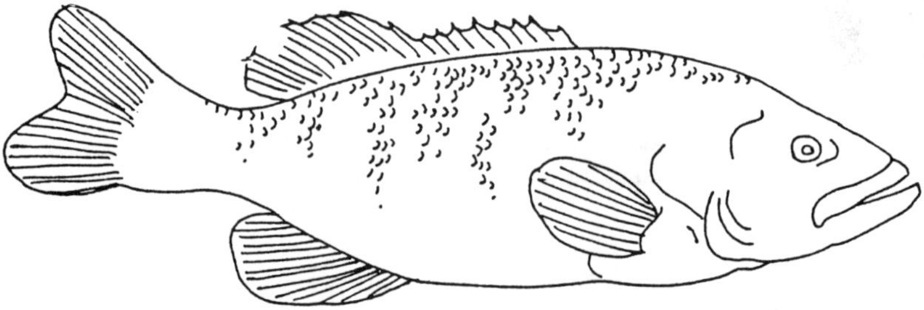

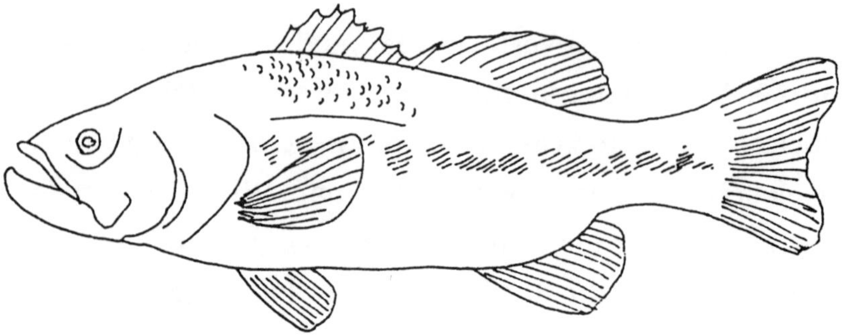

Where and When to Fish

Fish are usually found where there's plenty of food, where there's natural cover to hide in, and where the temperature of the water is comfortable for them. Different kinds of fish like different places. Some like deep water, some shallow. Some like cold water, some warmer water.

Good places to find many kinds of fish are around old stumps or floating logs near the water's edge. Rocky ledges and lily pads are also good fishing spots. Other places where fish usually cluster are by plants and weeds growing on the bottom and by rocks and deep holes in the water. Some fish also like to be near the outlets of small streams or brooks that flow into larger bodies of water.

Most fish stay away from places that are in direct sunlight. Shady places where trees hang over the water are usually fish-filled spots. The fish like the cool shade, and some feed on bugs that drop off the trees.

Almost any time of the day can be good for fishing. Many anglers claim that fishing in the early morning and the late evening is better than at midday. However, many big fish have been hooked between late morning and midafternoon. There really is no single best time for fishing.

Weather is a different matter. It can affect how the fish are biting. Many fish like to feed after rainstorms. The rain brings in a new supply of food, and so bottom-dwelling fish become more active. Fishing before a storm is good for other types of fish. Mild weather with partly cloudy skies usually means fishing will be good. Hot weather sends the fish deeper in the water.

Some Freshwater Fish

In this chapter, you'll learn about different kinds of freshwater fish, what they like for bait, and where they can be found. All of these fish can be hooked by still fishing or by casting.

CARP

Carp are big fish found in most rivers and lakes. They like to swim on muddy bottoms and in deep water.

They can be caught with artificial bait, but they enjoy natural bait best. These freshwater fish also like prepared bait such as dough balls and even kernels of corn strung in a row on a hook.

BOTTOM-DWELLING CARP

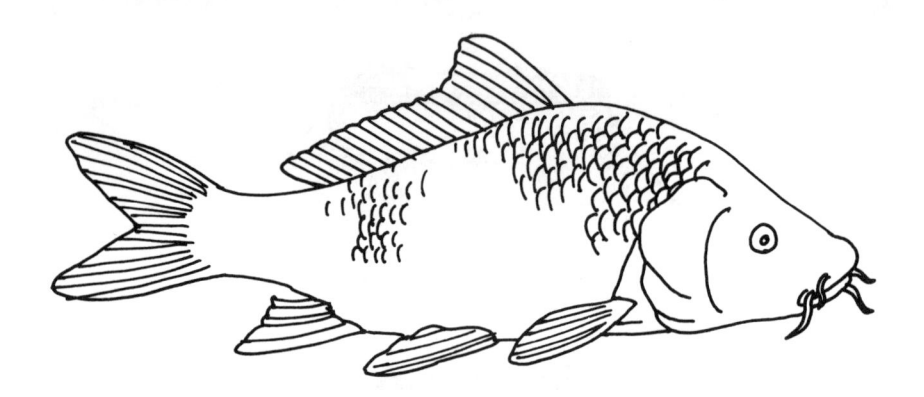

BLUEGILLS

Bluegills are small sunfish that often weigh under one pound. They feed by sight, which means bait has to look good to them. Crickets, grubs, worms, and small spinners or plugs are good bait for these fish.

BLUEGILL

Bluegills are found in most warm-water ponds, lakes, streams, and rivers. They usually stay close to cover such as brush, weeds, and rocks. If the weather is hot, they usually swim in water six to fifteen feet deep. If the weather is cool, they prefer shallow water close to shore.

Many other sunfish are similar to bluegills, such as redear, longear, and green sunfish. Many people refer to sunfish as bream.

PUMPKINSEED SUNFISH

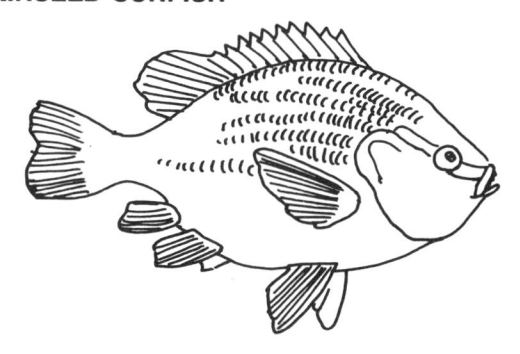

CATFISH

Some anglers think catfish are ugly. Others love to hook catfish because they make a great meal. Catfish are found just about any place where there's enough water for fishing.

Catfish like to swim on the bottom. Usually they are found in deep water holes. They also like places under fallen trees and where streams empty into deeper water.

Catfish prefer smelly bait. They will go after chicken liver, pieces of hot dogs, worms, and prepared bait such as cheesy chunks (see page 34).

CATFISH

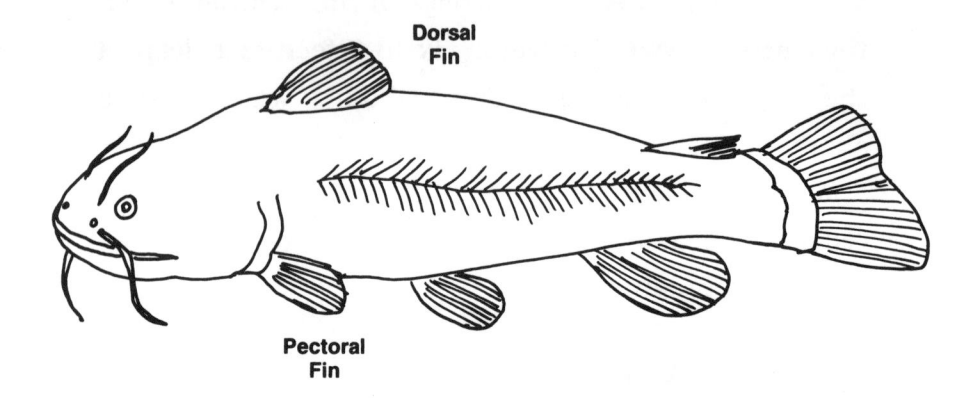

Dorsal Fin

Pectoral Fin

If you catch a catfish, do not worry about the whiskers when landing it. The whiskers can't hurt you. However, the catfish's sharp spines on its fins can hurt. Some catfish have slightly poisonous glands at the base of their pectoral fins (the ones at the lower front) and their dorsal fin (the one on the top). The poison isn't deadly to humans. But if a sharp fin breaks your skin, it can cause a painful wound. So handle a catfish carefully or use gloves.

SMALLMOUTH BASS

The smallmouth bass is another member of the sunfish family. This freshwater fish is famous for giving anglers a real tug of war when it's hooked.

Smallmouth bass like clear, cool water. Their favorite areas are rock and gravel, where they feed on crayfish and minnows. You'll also find them in deep water holes.

SMALLMOUTH BASS

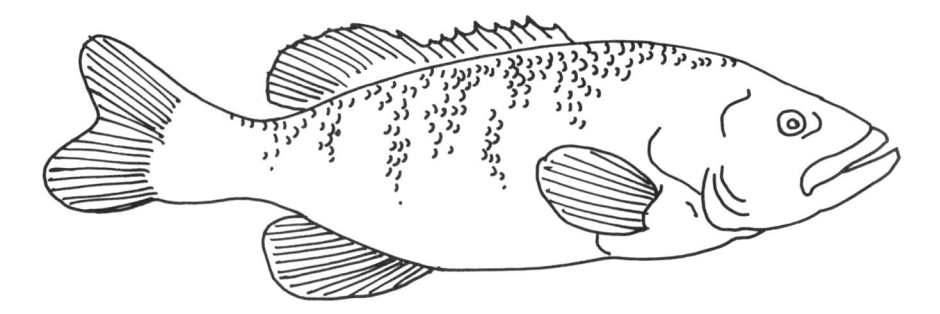

During midsummer and winter smallmouth bass will group together and feed in one spot.

Smallmouth bass will take both natural and artificial bait. Fishing for the smallmouth bass is usually best in the early morning, evening, or even at night.

LARGEMOUTH BASS

The largemouth bass is found in most large rivers, ponds, and lakes. It likes to be in quiet water and around cover such as logs and brush. It feeds on minnows, crayfish, frogs, bugs, and worms. Many people use artificial lures to fish for largemouth bass.

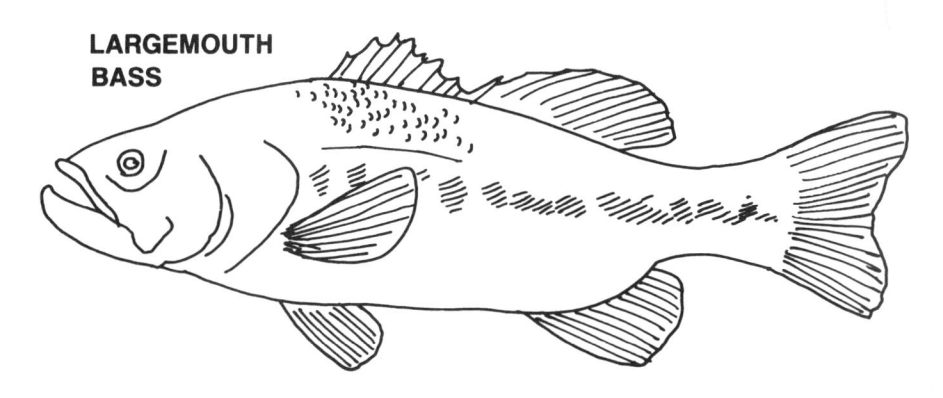

LARGEMOUTH BASS

PERCH

Perch is a freshwater fish that swims in schools in the slow-moving parts of rivers and streams as well as in lakes and ponds. Sometimes perch feed on bugs lying on the water's surface. Most of the time, however, they are found at depths of five to twenty feet.

Perch will take worms, crayfish, pieces of corn, and various insects such as crickets and grasshoppers for bait. The perch's favorite food, though, is a minnow. Occasionally, perch will also take prepared bait.

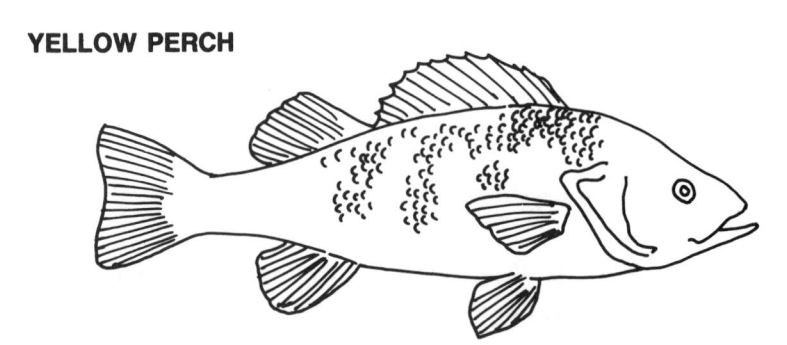

YELLOW PERCH

TROUT

Trout are found in cool, fresh water. You can catch them with live or artificial bait. Trout like worms, night crawlers, grasshoppers, and salmon eggs. You can also catch trout with flies, or small spinners or plugs.

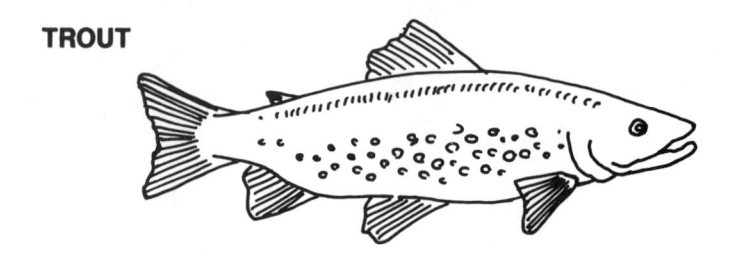

TROUT

Cleaning a Fish

Cleaning a fish is a job for an adult because it requires a sharp knife. Of course, you can help. Also, knowing the right way to clean a fish is something every angler should learn. To clean a fish, you'll need a sharp knife, a board, and clean water.

Lay the fish on a cutting board. Holding the fish's head, cut into the side of the fish just behind the gills. Cut deep but don't cut through the backbone. Slice down along the backbone to the tail. Do not cut into the rib cage. Cut the flesh away from the rib cage on each side, cutting through the stomach. Put the flesh (fillet) on the board, skin side down. Holding the fillet by the tail, cut the fillet off the skin.

Safe Fishing Fun

Fishing has a few unwritten rules all anglers should obey. One important one is this: The first person at a fishing spot has the right to fish it alone. Do not fish right next to another angler. Move on to a different spot. Another important rule is to be careful when casting (see page 47). Make sure no one is near you or right behind you. And finally, follow all state and local fishing regulations.

The sport of fishing is a lot of fun. But it's even more fun when it's done safely. Always be careful when you're near the water. Fish from an area where you can't fall into the water. If you fish near deep water or from a boat, always wear a life preserver. If you're on a boat, follow safe boating rules. And *never* go fishing by yourself. An adult should always accompany you.

By adhering to these simple guidelines, you'll enjoy fishing to the fullest. Catching a fish is a thrill that can't be matched. And even if you don't catch any, you'll be outdoors in the sunshine and fresh air. What better way is there to spend a leisurely day with family or friends? So good luck, anglers, and good fishing!

INDEX

Angler / 7
Bait / 22, 27-38
Bass / 58-59
Bluegills / 56-57
Bobbers / 14, 39-40
Carp / 55-56
Catfish / 57-58
Casting
    practice casting / 48-49
    with a close-face reel / 48-49
    with an open-face reel / 50-51
Cheesy Chunks / 34
Close-Face Spin-Casting Reel / 18
Dough Balls / 33-34
Equipment
    attaching / 23-25
    types of / 11-22
Fishing Line / 11-12
Flies / 36
Grasshoppers And Crickets
    baiting / 30
    finding / 30
Guides / 23
Hand Line / 16
Hooks
    kinds of / 12-13
    parts of / 12-13
    removing / 45-46
    snelled / 13
Jigs / 37
Knot, Palomar / 15-16
Landing The Fish / 42-43

Leader / 13
Minnows
    baiting / 31-32
    finding / 31
Net / 21
Open-Face Spinning Reel / 19
Perch / 60
Playing The Fish / 41-42
Pliers, Needle-Nose / 21
Plugs / 36-37
Pole / 17
Reel Bail / 19
Reels / 17-19
Regulations, Fishing / 22
Retrieve / 18
Rod / 19-20
Safety / 62-63
Setting The Hook / 41
Sinkers / 14
Snaps / 15
Spinnerbaits / 38
Spinners / 38
Spoons / 38
Swivels / 15
Tackle, Balanced / 21
Tackle Box / 21
Trout / 60
Weather / 54
Worms
    baiting / 28-29
    finding / 27-28